A Guide for Using

Harry Potter and the Sorcerer's Stone

and Other Harry Potter Books

in the Classroom

Based on the books written by
J.K. Rowling

This guide written by **Michelle Breyer, M.A.**

Teacher Created Materials, Inc.
6421 Industry Way
Westminster, CA 92683
www.teachercreated.com
©2002 Teacher Created Materials

Made in U.S.A.
ISBN 1-57690-638-8

Edited by
Cassandra K. Burton, M.S. Ed.
Eric Migliaccio

Illustrated by
Renée Christine Yates

Cover Art by
Lesley Palmer

Table of Contents

Introduction

A good book can touch our lives like a good friend. Within its pages are words and characters that can inspire us to achieve our highest ideals. We can turn to it for companionship, recreation, comfort, and guidance. It can also give us a cherished story to hold in our hearts forever.

In Literature Units, great care has been taken to select books that are sure to become good friends!

Teachers who use this literature unit will find the following features to supplement their own valuable ideas:

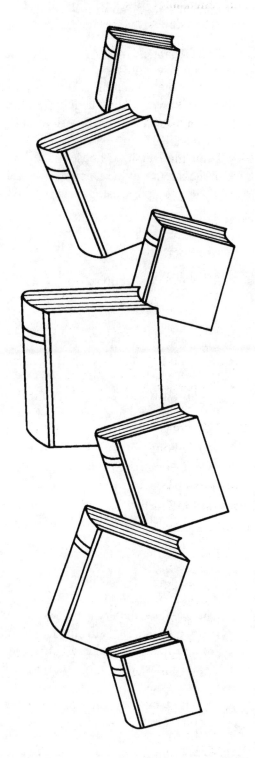

- Sample Lesson Plans

- Pre–reading Activities

- Biographical Sketch and Picture of the Author

- Book Summary

- Vocabulary Lists and Suggested Vocabulary Ideas

- Comprehension Questions and Suggested Comprehension Ideas

- Chapters grouped for study with each section which may include

  —a hands-on project

  —a cooperative learning activity

  —a cross-curricular connection

  —an extension into the reader's life

- Post–reading Activities

- Book Report Ideas

- Culminating Activity

- Three Different Options for Unit Tests

- Generic Activities for use with this unit or other books by J.K. Rowling: *Harry Potter and the Chamber of Secrets, Harry Potter and the Prisoner of Azkaban,* and *Harry Potter and the Goblet of Fire.*

- Bibliography

- Answer Key

We are confident that this unit will be a valuable addition to your planning, and we hope that as you use our ideas, your students will increase the circle of "friends" they have in books!

Sample Lesson Plans

Each of the lessons suggested below can take from one to several days to complete.

Lesson 1

- Introduce and complete some or all of the pre-reading activities found on page 5.
- Read "About the Author" (page 6) and the book summary (page 7) with your students.
- Introduce the Section 1 vocabulary list (page 8).

Lesson 2

- Read Chapters 1–4. As you read, place the vocabulary words in the context of the story and discuss their meanings. Do this for each section.
- Choose a vocabulary activity (page 9).
- Begin "Reader's Response Journals" (pages 14–15).
- Draw the Dursley's house (page 13).
- Write a letter to the Dursleys (page 16).
- Assign comprehension questions for Section 1 (page 10).
- Choose a comprehension activity (page 12)
- Optional activity: create life-sized characters (page 42).
- Introduce the Section 2 vocabulary list (page 8).

Lesson 3

- Read Chapters 5–7.
- Choose a vocabulary activity (page 9).
- Respond in journals to characters and events from this section (pages 14–15).
- Discuss ways we can feel included (page 17).
- Play the math game "Are You Knuts?" (page 18).
- Write about your first day of school (page 19).
- Assign comprehension questions for Section 2 (page 10).
- Choose a comprehension activity (page 12).
- Optional activity: "Design a Hogwarts Castle" (page 41).
- Introduce the Section 3 vocabulary list (page 8).

Lesson 4

- Read Chapters 8–11.
- Choose a vocabulary activity (page 9).
- Respond in journals to characters and events from this section (pages 14–15).
- Create a class monster book (page 20).
- Make up new sports games (page 21).
- Discuss facing a challenge (page 22).
- Assign comprehension questions for Section 3 (page 10).
- Choose a comprehension activity (page 12).
- Optional activity: examine Greek mythology (page 43).
- Introduce the Section 4 vocabulary list (page 8).

Lesson 5

- Read Chapters 12–14.
- Choose a vocabulary activity (page 9).
- Respond in journals to characters and events from this section (pages 14–15).
- Research and present your family tree (page 23).
- Create and describe team dragons (page 24).
- Imagine yourself in the Mirror of Erised (page 25).
- Assign comprehension questions for Section 4 (page 11).
- Choose a comprehension activity (page 12).
- Optional Activity: experiment with egg magic (page 39)
- Introduce the Section 5 vocabulary list (page 8).

Lesson 6

- Read Chapters 15–17.
- Choose a vocabulary activity (page 9).
- Respond in journals to characters and events from this section (pages 14–15).
- Design a new security system for Hogwarts (page 26).
- Debate the use of the Sorcerer's Stone (page 27).
- Learn about astronomy (page 28).
- Assign comprehension questions for Section 5 (page 11).
- Choose a comprehension activity (page 12).
- Optional Activity: create a time line (page 44).

Lesson 7

- Discuss any questions your students may have about the story (page 29).
- Assign book report projects (page 30).
- Begin work on the culminating activity (page 31) or optional culminating activities (pages 36–39).

Lesson 8

- Administer unit tests 1, 2, and/or 3 (pages 32–34).
- Discuss the students' opinions and enjoyment of the book.
- Provide a list of related reading for the students (page 46).

Before the Book

Before reading *Harry Potter and the Sorcerer's Stone*, it will be beneficial for the students to have a feel for the real geography and culture of England, as well as for the fantasy world in which the book is set. There are also some generic pre-reading ideas that can help students focus on the literature. Here are some activities that may work well in your class.

1. Predict what the story might be about by hearing the title.

2. Predict what the story might be about by looking at the cover illustration.

3. Discuss other books by J.K. Rowling that students may have heard about or read.

4. Individually or in small groups, list familiar books or stories that contain references to fantasy worlds and magic. These could be fairy tales, historical myths, or other works of literature. Discuss the elements of these stories that make them fantasy rather than real.

5. Write the word "Underdog" on the board. Have students describe what they think the word means. How does it apply to people, sports events, companies, and schools? Work together to list books in which the main character was the "underdog" and yet overcame great obstacles to become victorious in the end.

6. Answer these questions:

   ✦ How would it feel to be taken from your family at only one year old?

   ✦ What must it feel like not to know anything about your real parents and who you are?

   ✦ How would it feel to live in a house where you are despised and treated poorly?

   ✦ How could you leave this situation and make it on your own?

   ✦ What would you think if strange things seemed to "just happen" around you?

   ✦ How would it feel to discover you were famous in a different world?

   ✦ Is it right to break the rules if it is for a noble cause?

7. Discuss the concepts of destiny and fate. Have students discuss whether they think they have a hand in guiding their futures or if their futures are already planned for them. Discuss elements that influence their futures, such as family, school, obeying rules and laws, friends, and work ethic. How could a change in these elements influence their destinies? Which aspects of their futures can they control, and which aspects are out of their control?

8. President Kennedy once said, "Some men are born great, some achieve greatness, and some have greatness thrust upon them." Discuss as a class what this quote means and have students offer their opinions about people and their ability vs. destiny to become great or famous.

9. The main character in this story is able to face great obstacles and challenges with courage and character. Write descriptions or brainstorm ideas about what makes a person strong or courageous in the face of tragedy. Determine what the source of such strength might be—physical, emotional, psychological, or spiritual. Discuss these ideas as a class.

About the Author

J.K. (Joanne) Rowling (pronounced "rolling") began writing her first book when she was six and has not stopped writing since. Born in Chipping Sodbury General Hospital in England, J.K. grew up with her younger sister just outside of Bristol. Early storytelling adventures usually involved rabbits, since she and her sister badly wanted one for a pet. As she grew up, Rowling secretly wished to be a writer and collected names for characters and scribbled ideas for story plots. The "Potters," for example, were chums from their early neighborhood.

At the age of nine, her family moved to the countryside, where she and her sister explored the fields along the River Wye. Although the change of scenery was great fun, Rowling hated her new school, which was very small and old–fashioned. Her new teacher did not think highly of her potential, and young Joanne was scared of her. By the time she entered Wyedean Comprehensive, Rowling was quiet and freckle-faced with glasses. She loved her English classes, but she was horrible at sports. At lunchtime, she would tell her equally quiet and studious friends heroic stories. She continued to keep her passion for writing a secret.

Rowling excelled at other languages. She attended Exeter University after graduating as Head Girl from Wyedean and focused her studies on French. Her parents felt she would make an excellent bilingual secretary, but this was far from the truth. Instead of paying attention at meetings, she was scribbling down ideas for stories or names of characters so that she could type them up later when no one was looking. By the age of 26, discouraged with her progress, she gave up office work completely and traveled abroad to Portugal to teach English as a Foreign Language.

Rowling enjoyed teaching in the afternoons and evenings, for it gave her time in the mornings to write. By this time she had started her third novel (the first two were abandoned when she realized how bad they were) about a boy who found out he was a wizard and was sent off to wizard school. Home from Portugal, she was newly divorced, out of work, and living in an unheated Edinburgh flat with her infant daughter. To keep them both warm, she would wheel her daughter's stroller into a café and work out Potter plots on paper napkins. Her goal was to finish the novel and try to get it published before she began working as a French teacher.

Within a year, the Scottish Arts Council gave her a grant to finish the book. She was teaching French and writing on the side when she learned Bloomsbury (UK) and Scholastic Books was going to publish *Harry Potter and the Sorcerer's Stone.* After *Harry Potter* hit the stores and then the bestseller's lists, an American publisher bought the rights, paying her enough money that she was able to quit her teaching job to write full time—her life's ambition!

Harry Potter has won the British Book Award's Children's Book of the Year and the Smarties Prize with publications in England, France, Germany, Italy, Holland, Greece, Finland, Denmark, Spain, and Sweden. J.K. Rowling and her daughter try living a quiet life while she writes the rest of the Harry Potter books—seven in all, one for each of his years at Hogwarts.

Harry Potter and the Sorcerer's Stone

By J. K. Rowling

(Scholastic Inc., 1999)

Orphaned when he was only a baby, Harry Potter lives with his aunt and uncle, the Dursleys. A dull, Muggle (non-wizard) family, the Dursleys live at Number Four Privet Drive in Little Whining, England. Harry was rescued after Voldemort, a dark and evil sorcerer, had killed his wizard parents. Although the Dursleys are aware of Harry's magical potential, they attempt to raise him to be "normal" like their own precious son, Dudley. Showing little kindness, they make Harry live in a closet under the stairs. He wears only hand-me-down clothes and has never had even one birthday party. Harry's big break comes on his 11th birthday when a giant named Rubeus Hagrid arrives to take him to Hogwarts, the best wizard school in all of England.

From Hagrid, Harry learns that he is famous in the wizard world, having survived Voldemort's power. Hagrid takes Harry to Diagon Alley, a collection of wizard's shops, to buy the required items for a first–year student of wizardry. While on the train to Hogwarts, Harry meets Ron Weasley and Hermione Granger, who soon become his best friends. He also encounters his future nemesis, Draco Malfoy. Once at Hogwarts the students are greeted by the great wizard and headmaster, Albus Dumbledore. They are then sorted into houses and the magic begins.

Harry and his friends attend classes in the many fine wizard arts. Feeling overwhelmed by their new studies, they especially fear their potions teacher, Professor Snape. Besides being tormented by Draco Malfoy and Professor Snape, Harry encounters a mystery: he learns that Hagrid and Headmaster Dumbledore have hidden a secret package, and Harry fears Professor Snape may try to steal it.

The friends work to unravel the mystery of the package and learn of its connection to Voldemort. Making remarkable discoveries along the way, Harry and his friends thwart the sinister plot to steal the package. The book ends with Harry returning to the Dursleys for summer holiday, leaving the door open for the sequel, *Harry Potter and the Chamber of Secrets*.

Vocabulary Lists

On this page are vocabulary lists that correspond to each sectional grouping of chapters. Vocabulary activity ideas can be found on page 9 of this book.

Section 1 (Chapters 1–4)

chortled	ambling
gibber	knickerbockers
exasperated	annoying
irritably	rations
twanging	cloak
gingerly	vigorously
noble	Muggles

Section 2 (Chapters 5–7)

apothecary	transfiguration
minuscule	transparent
disgruntled	infernal
burnished	gawking
spindly	drawling
thronging	laden
swarthy	

Section 3 (Chapters 8–11)

ambition	berserk
hobbled	criticizing
jostled	keen
relieved	conjured
javelin	frantic
lumbered	spite
ensnaring	wheedled
triumphant	

Section 4 (Chapters 12–14)

taunting	petrified
fanatic	immortal
invisible	luminous
drawl	ushered
biased	eerie
suspend	bated
halfheartedly	

Section 5 (Chapters 15–17)

alibis	resolution
lingering	sweltering
confiscated	furor
feeble	tottered
imprecise	centaur
abysmal	mercy

The Dursley's House

Based on descriptions from the story, draw and color the items in the different rooms of the Dursley's house. Include as many items from the story as possible.

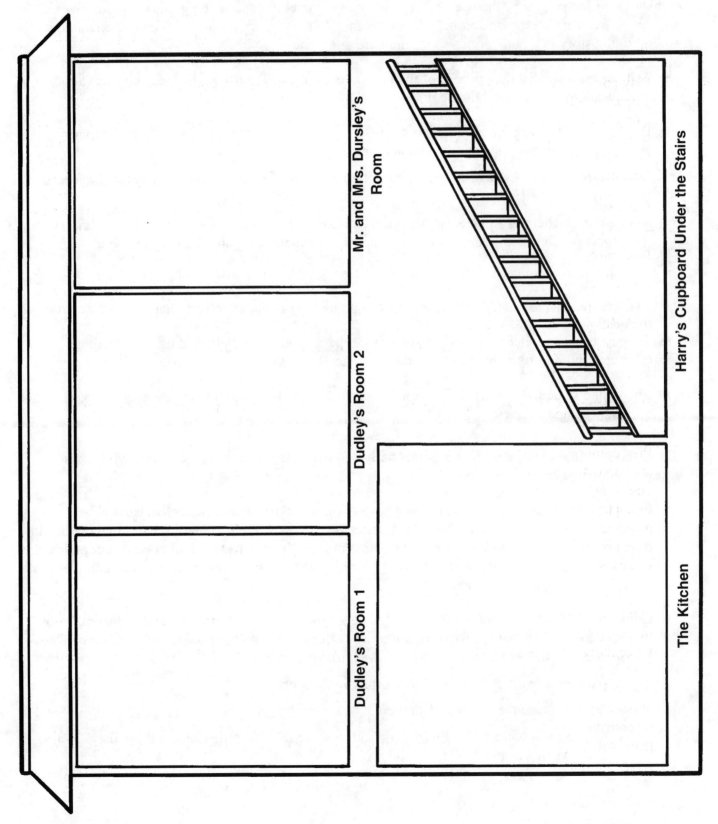

Reader's Response Journals

One reason avid readers are drawn to literature is because of what it does for them on a personal level. They are intrigued with how literature triggers their imaginations, what it makes them ponder, and how it makes them see and shape themselves. To aid your students in experiencing this for themselves, incorporate Reader's Response Journals in your plans. In these journals, students can be encouraged to respond to the story in a number of ways. Here are a few ideas:

✦ Tell the students that the purpose of the journal is to record their thoughts, ideas, observations, and questions as they read the book.

✦ Provide students with, or ask them to suggest, topics from the story that may stimulate writing. Here are some examples from the chapters in Section 1:

— Harry is forced to live in an unloving family. How do you think Harry feels? Have you ever felt like Harry?

— With the help of Rubeus Hagrid, Harry discovers he has a new life waiting for him. Have you ever left home to try something new? Was there someone there to help you?

✦ After the reading of each chapter, students can write one or more new things they learned.

✦ Ask the students to relate to the class their responses to certain events or characters in the story.

✦ Suggest to your students that they write diary-type responses to their reading by selecting a character and describing events from the character's point of view.

✦ Encourage students to bring their journal ideas to life by using them to create plays, stories, songs, art displays, and debates.

Allow students time to write in their journals daily. To evaluate the journals, you may wish to use the following guidelines:

✦ Personal reflections will be read by the teacher, but no corrections or letter grades will be assigned. Credit is given for effort, and all students who sincerely try will be awarded credit. If a grade is given for this type of entry, grade according to the number of journal entries completed. For example, if five journal assignments were made and the student conscientiously completes all five, then he or she should receive an "A."

✦ Constructive teacher responses should be made as you read the journals to let the students know that you are reading and enjoying their journals. Here are some types of responses that will please your journal writers and encourage them to write more:

— "You have really found what's important in the story!"

— "You've made me feel as if I'm there."

— "If you feel comfortable, I'd like for you to share this with the class. I think they'll enjoy your writing as much as I have."

Reader's Response Journal (cont.)

Keep this chart in your journal to record information about the different characters as you read each section. The chart can be used to help with some of the culminating activities.

Character	Description
Albus Dumbledore	
Professor McGonagall	
Professor Snape	
Professor Quirrel	
Professor Flitwick	
Professor Sprout	
Professor Binns	
Madam Pomfrey	
Rubeus Hagrid	
Argus Filch	
Harry Potter	
Ron Weasley	
Hermione Granger	
Draco Malfoy	
Neville Longbottom	
Vernon Dursley	
Petunia Dursley	
Dudley Dursley	

Letter Writing

In the opening chapter, Albus Dumbledore writes a letter to leave with baby Harry on the Dursleys' doorstep. He believes the Dursleys will explain everything to Harry when he's older, based on the contents of this letter. However, Professor McGonagall is doubtful and says, "Really, Dumbledore, you think you can explain all this in a letter?"

Pretend you are Albus Dumbledore and write the letter to Harry's aunt and uncle. Make sure you explain what happened, why Harry has been brought to them instead of a wizard family, and what their duties are as his new parents for the present and future time. Try to sound like the professor in your tone and use of vocabulary, and be sure to use proper letter format.

From the desk of

Hogwarts

Feeling Included

Harry has had an awkward upbringing without many friends. He confesses to Ron that he is anxious about not knowing as much as everyone else at school and having difficulty fitting in. When it comes time for Harry to be sorted into his house, he worries that he won't be picked at all, just like back home when picking teams. Everyone at some time feels like Harry—awkward, out of place, unliked, unpopular, clueless, or different.

List some times in your life when you have felt left out or awkward. These could be times at home, at school, or with your friends.

_____

_____

_____

_____

List the feelings you had when others treated you badly or didn't want you to join them.

_____

_____

_____

_____

Many people feel the way that you just described. Unfortunately, many adolescents turn to drugs, alcohol, gangs, crime, or suicide to deal with these feelings of loneliness and trying to fit in. Why do you think they do this? _____

_____

_____

_____

Think about times in your life when you may have caused bad feelings by teasing someone or excluding them from your group. Then list some ways that you can make other people feel good about their differences and feel included. Try to put these ideas into practice each day of your life.

_____

_____

_____

_____

Are You Knuts?

In Chapter 5, Harry goes shopping at Diagon Alley with his newly acquired wizard currency. Divide the class into teams of 4–6 students and play the game below using this magic money.

Materials (for each team)

◆ 1 sheet of lined paper divided into the columns shown. This will be the team bank statement.

◆ 2 dice

◆ pencil

Directions

1. Tell the class that they are going to work in the wizard world to earn money. The team that earns a gold galleon first will be the winning team.

2. Review wizard money by writing the following chart on the board:

> 29 bronze knuts = 1 silver sickle
>
> 17 silver sickles = 1 gold galleon

3. Explain to the class that each person on the team will take a turn rolling the dice, multiplying the two dice, and recording how many knuts they just earned on the bank statement. Each player's knuts are added onto the bank statement in the appropriate column.

4. As the game continues from player to player, knuts should be traded in for sickles. Once 17 sickles have been acquired, the team trades them in for a galleon and shouts, "We're ready for Diagon Alley!"

5. Play a practice game to make sure students understand how to record their dice rolls, knuts, and sickles.

6. Once students understand how to play, they can record their own knuts and play against the other members in their group.

Dice	Knuts	Sickles
2 x 4	8	
2 x 2	+ 4	
	12	
6 x 4	+ 24	
	36	
	- 29 ——→	Ⓢ
	7	
5 x 6	+ 30	
	37	
	- 29 ——→	Ⓢ
	8	
3 x 5	+ 15	
	23	

Extension: Use the items specified in Harry's letter from Hogwarts (pages 66–67) to create a shopping list. Brainstorm with students how much each item should cost (example, a wand is 7 Galleons). Write a price list on the board. Have students play for a designated amount of time to earn money and then use their money to buy items from the list. They need to deduct their spending from their bank statements. Play over an extended period of time and see if any student can purchase his or her entire shopping list.

First Day of School

J.K. Rowling captures Harry's excitement and nerves on his first day of school at Hogwarts. See how well you can describe your first day of school this year by brainstorming some ideas on the chart below. Then write a colorful and descriptive composition using forms of figurative language such as personification, metaphors, and similes. Include a catchy introduction and finish with a strong conclusion that reflects your overall feeling for the day.

See	_____
	_____
	_____
	_____

Hear	_____
	_____
	_____
	_____

Smell	_____
	_____
	_____
	_____

Touch	_____
	_____
	_____
	_____

Taste	_____
	_____
	_____
	_____

Create a Class Monster Book

Hogwarts and the wizard world are filled with mythical creatures and monsters. Discuss some of the creatures from the story and then design your own "monster" to be compiled in a book with others from the class. Follow the guidelines so that your monster will match up with the others when the pages are cut, then flipped to reveal crazy, mixed–up monsters.

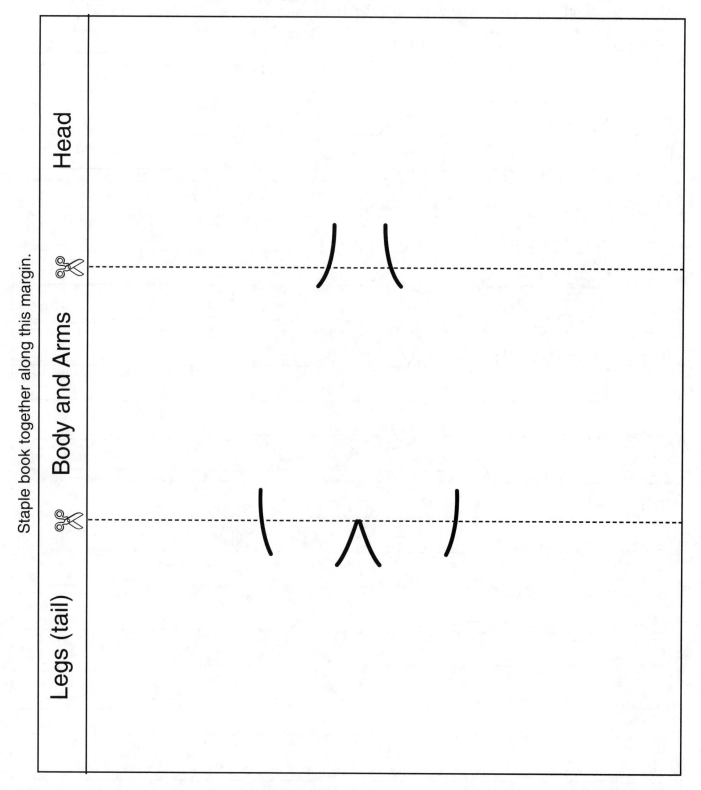

The New Sport

All around the wizard world fans follow the rivalry of their favorite Quidditch teams. Although the game is fictional, it does reflect some Muggle team games and rules. J.K. Rowling isn't the only person who can create a new game. Work together in a cooperative group to invent a new game that could be played at school. (No magic allowed!) Use the questions below to help get your group started. Once you have your game, teach the rest of the class how to play.

1. What equipment do you have available?_____

   _____

2. What equipment will your game use from this list? _____

   _____

3. Where do you play your game? (court, field, etc.) _____

4. How will you score points or goals? _____

   _____

5. Do you play in teams? _____

6. What are the different positions?_____

   _____

7. List the rules for your game. _____

   _____

   _____

8. What happens if someone breaks one of the rules? _____

   _____

9. How do you finally win the game? _____

   _____

10. What are you going to call your game? _____

Facing a Challenge

In the story, Harry is faced with many challenges: living with the Dursley's, going to Hogwarts, chasing after Malfoy and the Remembrall on his first broom ride, accepting a wizard's duel, and fighting off a mountain troll. How Harry chooses to face these challenges greatly affects their outcome and his future.

Think of a time in your life when you were faced with a challenge. It could be trying something new, dealing with a family crisis, fighting against peer pressure, or any other event that you felt was especially challenging. Use this page to organize your information. Be sure the reader understands what happened during the incident, when and where it happened, how you chose to face the challenge (i.e., fight, ignore it, or seek help), the reactions and feelings of the people involved in the incident, and why this incident was especially challenging to you.

Introduction (Opening Statement)—The opening statement lets the reader know what you are going to write about. You can restate the prompt, adding your event, or you can be creative and start with some action from your story. Make sure it is clear that you understand the prompt.

_____

_____

_____

_____

_____

Specific Supporting Details (Sequence Statements)—This is the majority of your piece. It must include a clear sequence of what happened, the setting of the event, and the reactions and feelings of the characters involved. Write a brief description of the sequence.

_____

_____

_____

_____

_____

Conclusion (Summary Statement)—Wrap it up by describing at least three reasons why this event was especially challenging. End with a strong closing statement.

_____

_____

_____

_____

_____

Presenting Your Family Tree

In Chapter 12, Harry gets his first glimpse of his family in the Mirror of Erised. Try your hand at uncovering your family's past by researching your family heritage and presenting a "family tree" to your class. First, write your name on the trunk of the tree. Then, duplicate the leaves below. Add the name of a relative above the line on the leaf and his/her relation to you below the line. Place the leaves on the appropriate branch of your family tree. Try to record at least three generations.

During the presentation of the different generations, describe in detail at least one family member who you find particularly interesting. If possible, bring in photographs to show to the class.

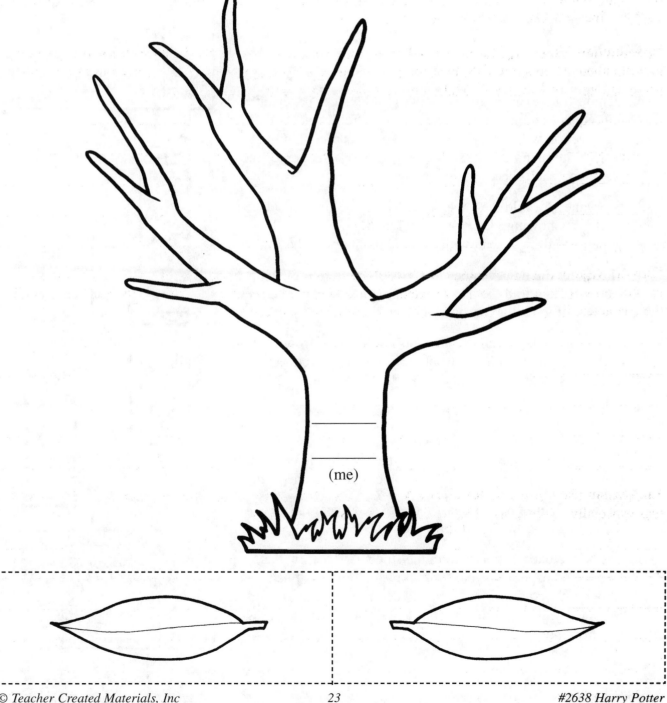

(me)

Team Dragons

Hagrid has always wanted a dragon, and to Harry's dismay he finally gets his wish. Team up students to hatch some interesting and ferocious dragons of their own by following the directions below. This activity works best if you model each step and remind students not to peek at what has been drawn.

Materials (for each student)

✦ one sheet of 12" x 18" (30.4 cm x 45.6 cm) white construction paper

✦ scissors

✦ colored markers

✦ lined paper for description

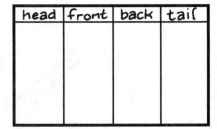

Directions

1. Divide students into groups of four.

2. Demonstrate to each student how to fold his/her paper into four equal sections. Label each section. Tell students that each section will represent a portion of the dragon and that each group member will be drawing only one section of the dragon on each sheet of paper.

3. Everyone will fold the paper so that only the first "head" section is showing. Using the black marker, instruct all students to draw a head with the neck going onto the fold.

4. Make sure the neck can be clearly seen going into the next section. Then fold the paper so that the head cannot be seen and pass it to the next group member.

5. Using the neck guidelines, students all draw the front portion of the dragon, including a front foot. Features such as scales and wings can be added as long as they stay in the section.

6. Draw body guidelines into the next section, fold over, and pass to the next member.

7. Using the guidelines, students draw the rear of the body and rear foot in the third section. Add other details as needed.

8. Draw guidelines onto the last section, fold over, and pass to the last member who will draw the tail.

9. Lastly, the paper is returned to the student who drew the head. Unfold the paper to reveal the completed dragon. Each student will color, add details, and describe the dragon and its personality. Cut out the dragons and display them along with the descriptions.

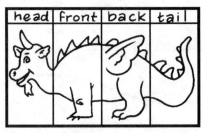

The Mirror of Erised

Professor Dumbledore explained that the Mirror of Erised showed people nothing more nor less than the deepest, most desperate desire of their hearts. Harry pictured his family surrounding him, while Ron saw himself standing alone with honors. What do you think you would see if you were to gaze into this magical looking glass? Draw a picture below and describe what you see.

_____

_____

_____

_____

_____

Security Systems Incorporated

Harry discovers an intricate security system guarding the Sorcerer's Stone. However, he and his friends are able to reach the stone with a bit of research and help. Imagine you are hired to protect the Sorcerer's Stone and needed to advise each of the teachers on their spells. What kind of security system would you design?

Alone, with a partner, or in a small group, write a security measure for each of the staff members listed below. It must be different from the spell in the book. On a separate sheet of paper, draw a map showing your security system in place.

❖ Hagrid (resident giant and keeper of monsters) _____

_____

❖ Professor Sprout (Herbology teacher) _____

_____

❖ Professor Flitwick (Charms teacher) _____

_____

❖ Professor McGonagall (Transfiguration teacher) _____

_____

❖ Professor Snape (Potions teacher) _____

_____

❖ Professor Quirrel (Defense Against the Dark Arts teacher) _____

_____

❖ Professor Dumbledore (Supreme Wizard)_____

_____

Debate the Sorcerer's Stone

In the final chapter, Harry and Professor Dumbledore discuss the merits of the Sorcerer's Stone. Although Harry believes it to be a wonderful invention, Dumbledore disagrees, claiming, "As much money and life as you could want! The two things most human beings would choose above all—the trouble is, humans do have a knack of choosing precisely those things that are worst for them." Have your class debate the pros and cons of acquiring the Sorcerer's Stone.

1. Divide the class into two groups. Have one group promote the merits of the Stone, while the other group will point out its drawbacks.

2. Assign each group a leader to facilitate the discussion and a secretary to record supporting arguments and examples. Allow ample time for groups to research, discuss, and prioritize their arguments. Make sure all students have had an opportunity to participate and understand their positions and points.

3. On the day of the debate, have each group sit across from each other in the room. Tell students that you will be calling on them randomly, so it is important that each member of the group is prepared to speak.

4. Review the speaking order below before beginning the actual debate. Tell students they will have three minutes to argue their point. Assign a student to be the timekeeper.

5. Flip a coin to decide which group will speak first. Then guide the debate as follows:

    ✦ Teacher presents the subject for debate and calls on a random speaker from group #1.

    ✦ Group #1 presents a supporting argument for their position.

    ✦ Group #2 refutes or tries to disclaim the point made by group #1.

    ✦ Another speaker from group #2 then presents a supporting argument for their position.

    ✦ Group #1 refutes the point made by group #2.

    ✦ Group #1 presents a supporting argument for their position.

6. The debate continues in this fashion—presenting a point, refuting the point, presenting a new point—until both groups have run out of points to support their position.

7. At the end of the debate take a secret poll to see which group was the most convincing. Discuss the outcome of the vote and the techniques used during the debate.

8. If desired, have students write persuasive essays defending their positions.

Astronomy

The Centaurs from the forbidden forest are all interested in the night sky and the predictions told by the stars. Most people have seen the constellation of stars called the Big Dipper, yet there are many other constellations, or patterns of stars identified in the sky. Try your hand at the study of the stars by completing one or more activities below.

Make a Model of a Constellation—Although a constellation appears in a pattern, the stars may actually be very different in size and millions of light years apart. When seen from an angle other than from Earth, the stars may not form a pattern at all. To demonstrate this, make a model using a cardboard box, scissors, black paint or paper, aluminum foil, black thread, and tape.

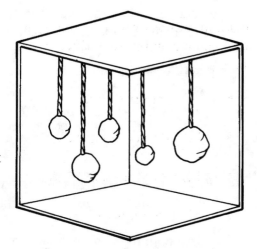

1. Cut off two sides of the box as shown.

2. Cover the inside of the box with black paint or paper.

3. Cut five different lengths of thread to hang your stars.

4. Roll some foil into five hanging balls by first wrapping it around the thread and then forming it into a ball. Make the balls different sizes.

5. Turn the box upside down and tape the hanging balls so that they make a pattern when viewed from one viewpoint.

6. Observe the pattern from the front of the box, then observe the balls from the side. How does changing your point of view affect the pattern that you see?

Moving Stars—The sun seems to move around the sky as Earth rotates; the stars at night do the same. Use a drinking straw as a telescope to measure the movements of a star over a period of time.

1. Look through a straw at a bright star. Steady the straw against a fence or other object and tape it in place so that you can still see through it.

2. Make a chart like the one below to record the movement and times.

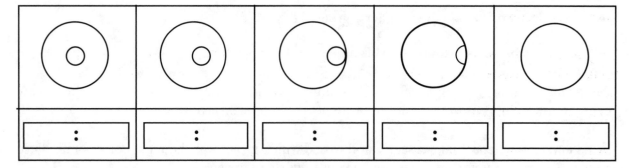

3. Record your starting time with the star in the middle of your straw. Then record each of the other movements on the chart. How long did it take for your star to move out of view? Do some stars travel faster than others?

Astrological Signs—The Greeks believed that the Centaur was put into the sky by Zeus, the king of the gods. Research the other astrological constellations and see if you can locate them in your night sky.

Any Questions?

When you finished reading *Harry Potter and the Sorcerer's Stone*, did you have some questions that were left unanswered? Write some of your questions here. _____

_____

_____

_____

Work in groups or by yourself to prepare possible answers for some or all of the questions you have asked above and those written below. When you have finished your predictions, share your ideas with the class.

- ✦ How is Voldemort able to convince Professor Quirrel to join his cause?

- ✦ Where do you think Voldemort contacts Professor Quirrel?

- ✦ Where do you think Voldemort has gone?

- ✦ Do you think he will return to Hogwarts?

- ✦ Why do you think Voldemort wants to kill Harry in the first place?

- ✦ Why do you think Professor Snape hates Harry's father?

- ✦ How do you think Harry's father saved Snape's life when they were at Hogwarts?

- ✦ Why doesn't Professor Snape warn Harry about Professor Quirrel?

- ✦ What ever becomes of the Mirror of Erised?

- ✦ Do you think Professor Dumbledore knows all of these things would happen to Harry? Do you think he has a master plan for Harry and Hogwarts that only he knows about?

- ✦ What do you think will happen to Harry once he goes back home?

- ✦ Do you think Harry will get to visit Ron or Hermione during summer vacation?

- ✦ What do you think will happen to Harry next year when he returns to Hogwarts as a second-year student?

Book Report Ideas

After you have finished *Harry Potter and the Sorcerer's Stone*, choose a method of reporting on it that appeals to you. Your book report may be an idea of your own or one of the suggestions below.

✧ **The Eyes Have It**

Do a visual report by making a model of a scene from the story, drawing or sculpting a likeness of one or more of the characters or crafting an important symbol from the book.

✧ **Time Capsule**

Provide people in the future with reasons to read *Harry Potter and the Sorcerer's Stone*. Inside a time-capsule-shaped design, neatly write your reasons. You may "bury" the capsule after you have shared it with your class.

✧ **Come to Life!**

A size-appropriate group prepares a scene from the story for dramatization, acts it out, and relates the significance of the scene in the context of the entire book. Costumes and props will add to the dramatization!

✧ **Into the Future**

Predict what might happen if *Harry Potter and the Sorcerer's Stone* were to continue. You may write it as a story in a narrative form, a dramatic script, or do a vista display.

✧ **Guess Who or What**

Give a series of clues about a character from the story in a general-to-specific order. After each clue, someone may try to guess the character. After all of the clues, if the subject cannot be guessed, the reporter may tell the class. The reporter then does the same for an event in the book, and then for an important object or symbol.

✧ **A Character Comes to Life!**

Suppose one of the characters in the book comes to life and walks into your home or classroom. This report gives the character's point of view as he or she sees, hears, feels, and experiences the world in which you live.

✧ **Sales Talk**

This is an advertisement to "sell" *Harry Potter* to one or more specific groups. You decide on the group to target and the sales pitch you will use. Include some illustrations in your presentation.

✧ **Literary Interview**

This report is done in pairs. One student will pretend to be a character in the story and steep him/herself completely in that character's persona. The other student will play the role of a radio or television interviewer, providing the audience with interesting insights into the character's life and personality. It is the responsibility of the partners to create meaningful questions and appropriate answers.

✧ **Dust Jacket Design**

Design a dust jacket for the novel. Include the title, author, and an important scene on the cover and a book summary on the inside flaps. On the back of the dust jacket, include a teaser (a hint at the plot that will make people want to read the book), as well as quotable recommendations for the book (such as "*The New York Times* calls it the best novel ever!").

Response

Explain the meaning of these quotes from *Harry Potter and the Sorcerer's Stone*.

Note to the teacher: Choose the appropriate number of quotes to which your students should respond.

1. "'Yes,' said Dumbledore. 'He'll have that scar forever.'" *(chapter 1)*

2. "The room held no sign at all that another boy lived in the house, too." *(chapter 2)*

3. "The problem was, strange things often happened around Harry and it was just no good telling the Dursleys he didn't make them happen." *(chapter 2)*

4. "Today he'd rather be back in his cupboard with that letter than up here without it." *(chapter 3)*

5. "Harry wished he had about eight more eyes." *(chapter 5)*

6. "'Well, I say your father favored it—it's really the wand that chooses the wizard, of course.'" *(chapter 5)*

7. "He didn't know what he was going to—but it had to be better than what he was leaving behind." *(chapter 6)*

8. "Harry thought that none of the lessons he'd had so far had given him as much to think about as tea with Hagrid." *(chapter 8)*

9. "'I want to hear you're training hard, Potter, or I may change my mind about punishing you.'" *(chapter 9)*

10. "But from that moment on, Hermione Granger became their friend." *(chapter 10)*

11. "'Blasted thing,' Snape was saying, 'How are you supposed to keep your eyes on all three heads at once?'" *(chapter 11)*

12. "'Mom?' he whispered, 'Dad?'" *(chapter 12)*

13. "'It does not do to dwell on dreams and forget to live, remember that.'" *(chapter 12)*

14. "He'd really done something to be proud of now—no one could say he was just a famous name anymore." *(chapter 13)*

15. "Only Ron stood by him." *(chapter 15)*

16. "'A lot of the greatest wizards haven't got an ounce of logic, they'd be stuck in here forever.'" *(chapter 16)*

17. "'After all, to the well-organized mind, death is but the next great adventure.'" *(chapter 17)*

18. "'Fear of a name increases fear of the thing itself.'" *(chapter 17)*

19. "It was the best evening of Harry's life, better than winning at Quidditch, or Christmas, or knocking out mountain trolls . . . he would never, ever forget tonight." *(chapter 17)*

Conversations

Work in groups to write and perform the conversation that might have occurred in one of the following situations. If you prefer, you may make up your own conversation for characters from *Harry Potter and the Sorcerer's Stone*.

✦ Albus Dumbledore converses with Petunia Dursley when dropping off Harry as a baby.

✦ Harry, Dudley, and Piers discussing Dudley's birthday on the way to the zoo.

✦ Harry telling his aunt and uncle how he feels about his life with them and Hogwarts.

✦ Harry and Ron on the train describing their lives and hopes for their futures at Hogwarts.

✦ Harry and Hagrid discussing the meaning of Harry's wand after leaving the shop.

✦ Professor Snape and Quirrel converse at the opening banquet.

✦ Harry confronts Snape to ask why he hates him so much.

✦ Ron, Hermione, and Malfoy discuss Harry's fate with Professor McGonagall after his first unauthorized broom flight.

✦ Malfoy trying to convince Filch to go to the trophy room and catch Harry looking for a duel.

✦ Ron and Harry advise Hermione on how to make friends.

✦ Ron, Harry, and Neville talk about the first Quidditch game.

✦ Harry speaks with his Mom and Dad in the Mirror of Erised.

✦ Harry, Ron, and Hermione call Nicholas Flamel to discuss the Sorcerer's Stone.

✦ Ron, Hermione, and Albus Dumbledore relive the quick victory over Hufflepuff.

✦ Harry and Hermione try to get out of trouble with Filch after releasing the dragon.

✦ Malfoy tries to convince Professor McGonagall that Hagrid really did have a dragon.

✦ Hagrid and the centaurs discuss the future foretold by the planets.

✦ Hermione saves Ron from the chessboard after escaping the potion fire.

✦ Quirrel has a last conversation with Voldemort before he dies.

✦ Harry describes his year at Hogwarts to the Dursleys.

Book Summaries for Other Harry Potter Adventures

✧ *Harry Potter and the Chamber of Secrets*

Warned by a bug-eyed house elf not to return to school, Harry barely makes it to Hogwarts by flying Mr. Weasley's enchanted car with Ron. As if landing in the Whomping Willow wasn't bad enough, the year begins with someone casting a spell on the caretaker's cat and leaving the message, "The Chamber of Secrets has been opened. Enemies of the Heir Beware!" Harry, Ron, and Hermione are soon investigating the mysterious old legend that claims a monster lives in the "Chamber of Secrets" and seeks to kill all Mudbloods at the school. With further attacks terrorizing the school, Harry finds himself the chief suspect for the evil doings. Through many twists and turns involving a conceited and inept professor, a crying ghost, giant spiders, and a loyal Pheonix, Harry discovers the secret of the chamber. Once inside he defeats the monster and Lord Voldemort, the true culprit of the attacks, who had returned to Hogwarts through an enchanted diary for the sole purpose of defeating Harry.

✧ *Harry Potter and the Prisoner of Azkaban*

Sirius Black—the infamous prisoner of Azkaban fortress—has escaped. All of London—magicals and Muggles alike—are searching in fear for this dreaded villain believed to be the right-hand man of Lord Voldemort. Meanwhile, due to a magical blow-up at the Dursleys', Harry finds himself on the lam and possibly expelled from his third term at Hogwarts for misuse of magic. Yet, to his astonishment, he is personally escorted to Diagon Alley and then to Hogwarts by none other than the Minister of Magic. Once at school, Harry discovers that his preferred treatment is due to the fact that he is considered the prime target for Sirius Black. So, while Hermione doubles her class load, Ron and other students frequent the local town Hogsmeade, and Hagrid tries his hand at teaching a class on magical creatures, Harry does his best to keep his cool under the watchful eyes of the dementors and his recurring nightmares. Finally, with help from his friends, a new Dark Arts teacher (and part-time werewolf), a magical marauder's map, and the invisibility cloak, Harry learns the true identity of Sirius Black and the true villain, Peter Pettigrew. Yet, in the end, Pettigrew escapes and Sirius is again falsely accused. It is only with the help of Hermione's potion and Hagrid's Hippogriff that Sirius is able to flee Hogwarts and return again in future adventures.

✧ *Harry Potter and the Goblet of Fire*

Harry is now 14 and in his fourth term at Hogwarts. He ends the summer by participating in the Quidditch World Cup championships, yet his scar has been burning. For Lord Voldemort is gaining strength with the help of Wormtail (Peter Pettigrew) and Barty Crouch. Furthermore, at the World Cup, rioting wizards known as the Death Eaters attack some innocent Muggles and conjure the Dark Mark—a sure sign of Voldemort's return to power. Besides worrying about Voldemort, all of Hogwarts is abuzz about the Triwizard Tournament: two other wizarding schools have come to Hogwarts to compete. Quidditch matches have been suspended for the year so students can prepare to compete for a position on their school's team. Through many plot twists and turns, Harry makes the Hogwarts team, wins the Triwizard Championship for Hogwarts, and escapes harm from Voldemort in a blazing duel of wands. However, the story ends with many loose ends and questions of loyalty—especially from the Minister of Magic. It seems there may be an all-out wizard war brewing in books to come!

The Hogwarts Seal

Throughout the Harry Potter stories you learned about the four houses at Hogwarts and the types of students who were sorted into the different houses based on their characteristics. Use the chart below to describe the four houses. Use the pattern on page 37 to design the Hogwarts seal.

House Name	Color	Animal Symbol	Characteristics or Traits	Students, Teachers, and Ghosts associated with the house
GRYFFINDOR				
HUFFLEPUFF				
RAVENCLAW				
SLYTHERIN				

36

The Hogwarts Seal *(cont.)*

Setting Map

Include the class in designing a bulletin board display depicting the setting of the Harry Potter stories. Use the guidelines from below and information from the books to create the setting map. Assign individuals or groups to create different aspects of the display. Have students research each book and its chapters to record information about the setting. Using construction paper, markers, and crayons, cut and paste the different features onto the map. Be sure to label them with appropriate headings.

Include the following features on your setting map from the first book and add to the list as you read further stories:

Hogwarts Grounds to the North

✦ Hogwarts Castle on a cliff next to the lake

✦ Hogwarts school grounds and green houses

✦ the forbidden forest

✦ Hagrid's hut

✦ the Quidditch field

Area Between Hogwarts and the Muggles

✦ train track for the Hogwarts Express

✦ mountains

✦ forest

✦ dark green hills

✦ twisting rivers

✦ woods

✦ fields of cows and sheep

✦ Muggle towns

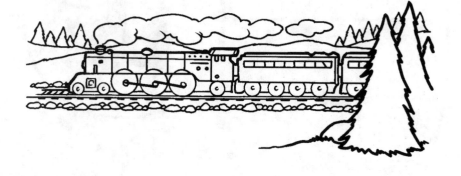

Muggle Area to the South

✦ Mr. Dursley's factory, Grunnings

✦ Privet Drive and the Dursley's house, Number Four

✦ Harry and Dudley's old school

✦ the zoo

✦ London

✦ Diagon Alley and Gringotts (the wizard bank)

✦ King Cross Station, platform nine and three-quarters

Egg Magic

Harry and his classmates are getting better and better at their spells and potions. Amaze your friends and family with a few of these scientific magic tricks!

✧ Obedient Eggs

For these tricks you will need a raw egg and a hard-boiled egg that has been kept upright while cooking. Tell your audience that you have two pet eggs that love to perform. (You can give them names).

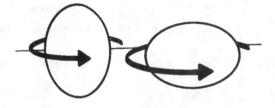

Trick #1—Have one person from the audience come up for the demonstration and hand him or her the raw egg. Have him or her try to spin their egg on its end without falling over. It won't. Then, stand your hard-boiled egg on its end, say some hocus pocus, and command it to dance. Spin the egg and watch it twirl on end.

Trick #2—Take the raw egg and spin it vigorously on its side. Gently stop it with one finger, then let go and command the egg to spin again. It will!

Trick #3—Next, spin the hard-boiled egg on its side and command it to "stand." If the yolk has been cooked in the bottom it should spin in an upright position.

✧ The Floating Egg

This experiment is based on the property of density. Objects will float in water when they are less dense than the water.

1. Take a hard-boiled egg and slide it carefully into a glass of water. It will sink because it is denser than the water.

2. Wave your hand over the water sprinkling in magic ingredients like eye of newt and frog gizzard (really it's salt!) and say some magic words to make the egg float.

3. The egg will float because the salt makes the water denser.

4. To suspend the egg halfway, slowly add fresh water to the glass.

✧ Egg Pressure

Here is a little trick using the property of air pressure. You will need a peeled and wet hard-boiled egg, some paper, a match or lighter, and an 8-ounce (240 ml) glass baby bottle. Twist some paper tightly to make a small torch. Say some magic words, light the paper, and drop it into the bottle. Immediately place the wet egg, tapered end down, onto the bottle. Slowly the egg should be sucked in.

Note: This last activity is best done as a teacher demonstration.

Loyalty

Most people consider loyalty to be a positive and admirable character trait. J.K Rowlings uses loyalty as a theme throughout the Harry Potter adventures to illustrate good overcoming evil. Harry is loyal to his friends; loyal to his family (his real mom and dad, that is); loyal to his House, the Gryffindors; and loyal to Albus Dumbledore and Hogwarts.

Do you think loyalty is admirable or important for one's character? Follow the directions below to write a persuasive essay about loyalty.

1. Choose a specific type of loyalty to write about: loyalty towards your family, friends, school, a sports team, country, your own beliefs, etc.

2. Choose a position for or against being loyal.

3. Outline your essay using the following format:

   A. Opening statement/thesis (describe the type of loyalty you are discussing and your position)

   B. Persuasive reason #1 and supporting details

   C. Persuasive reason #2 and supporting details

   D. Persuasive reason #3 and supporting details

   E. Closing statement/conclusion (briefly restate your reasons for your position and give a strong closing statement)

4. Use the following writing process to compose your essay:

   1. pre-write and/or outline
   2. rough draft
   3. edit
   4. revise
   5. final draft

5. If desired, share your essay with the class by reading it or presenting it as a persuasive speech.

Design a Hogwarts Castle

Imagine their astonishment as Harry and his new friends get their first glimpse of the Hogwarts Castle perched on top of a hill next to a lake. Make your own castle of wizardry by following the directions below.

Materials

- ✦ 1 sheet of light tan or gray construction paper
- ✦ 1 sheet of blue construction paper
- ✦ pencil
- ✦ books with examples of castles
- ✦ scissors and glue
- ✦ colored markers
- ✦ thin, black permanent marker

Directions

1. Examine several examples of castles from books. Notice the different architectural features and textures of the building materials.

2. Draw a castle on the sheet of tan or gray construction paper with pencil. Divide the castle into interesting sections, with towers, turrets, arches, windows, and doors.

3. Outline your castle with the permanent marker and begin adding details and textures, such as stones, wood, shingles, spider webs, stained glass, flags, banners, archways, gargoyles, and hinges.

4. Color the windows and doors of the castle along with any other architectural features you want to stand out.

5. Cut open the doors and windows leaving one side for a hinge. Then cut out the castle.

6. Glue the castle onto the blue paper leaving the doors and windows free.

7. Draw ghosts and other Hogwarts items inside the door and window openings.

8. Display your Hogwarts Castles around the classroom.

Life-Sized Characters

J.K. Rowling has a wonderful knack for making each character come to life. Divide the class into groups to illustrate and describe all or some of these colorful characters: Mr. Vernon Dursley, Mrs. Petunia Dursley, Dudley Dursley, Harry Potter, Ron Weasley, Hermione Granger, Professor Albus Dumbledore, Professor Severus Snape, Professor McGonagall, Argus Filch, Madame Pomfrey, Gilderoy Lockhart, Sirius Black, Draco Malfoy and the giant, Rubeus Hagrid.

Materials (for each group)

- ✦ two sheets of lined writing paper

- ✦ two sheets of white butcher paper, each about 6 feet (180 cm) long

- ✦ several sheets of colored construction paper

- ✦ markers, crayons, and pencils

- ✦ scissors and glue

Directions

1. Assign each group a character and an area in the classroom to work.

2. Students begin researching their character by listing on the first sheet of lined paper descriptive quotes and page numbers from the book. Quotes can be dialogue or descriptions about how the character appears, acts, or how other characters feel about him or her.

3. After finding an acceptable amount of information, the groups will each write a descriptive paragraph about their character on the second sheet of lined paper.

4. Using the descriptions, each group will plan how they want their character to pose and look.

5. Choose appropriate students to trace around on the butcher paper. For example, taller students should be the adults, the teacher may need to be Hagrid, and the smaller students can be Harry and Dudley. Remind students that these outlines are only a guide to help with proportion.

6. Once traced in pencil, modify and refine the outlines to better portray the character's attributes.

7. When students are satisfied with the outlines, they can draw the details.

8. Use construction paper to create clothes, shoes, hair, and facial features, and glue them onto the character.

9. When the character is completed, glue it to the second sheet of butcher paper to add strength for hanging.

10. After the glue has dried, cut the character out, leaving a small border around the outline.

11. Display each of the characters along with their descriptions around the classroom. If desired, have each group present its character to the class by reading his or her description.

Greek Mythology

Harry and his friends encounter a three-headed guard dog in *Harry Potter and the Sorcerer's Stone*. This dog was none other than Cerberus, a creature from Greek mythology. Below is a description of Cerberus, along with those of a few other mythological monsters. Read the descriptions and then complete one or more of the activities listed at the bottom.

✧ Cerberus

This three-headed dog was said to guard the gates to Tartarus. Here, spirits of the dead were sent to be judged by Hades, the king of the Underworld. Cerberus would stand guard and nip at the heels of those souls unwilling to enter and devour spirits who attempted to leave. One of the most famous tales about Cerberus involved the great hero Hercules and his 12 labors. Cerberus was also outwitted by the hero Orpheus, who traveled to Hades to retrieve his true love.

✧ Medusa

The youngest and most famous of the Gorgons, Medusa had a mass of living snakes for hair; a broad, flat face; fangs; and a tongue that lolled out like a lizard's. Anyone who looked at her face would be turned to stone. Some say it was magic in her eyes, and some claim she was so terrible one just froze on the spot. Perseus was able to defeat Medusa by using his shield like a mirror, thus escaping her direct gaze.

✧ Centaur

When the Greeks first domesticated horses they never dreamed of riding one—that is, until they encountered the Scythians north of the Black Sea. These wild horsemen could ride and shoot arrows from horseback. It is from tales of these horsemen that the legend of the Centaur grew. The legend claimed that the Centaur had the upper torso of a man and the body of a horse. Centaurs were barbaric, eating raw meat and wine until it drove them into a killing frenzy. However, there was one exception: Chiron. He was civilized and a skilled teacher of such famous students as Hercules, Achilles, and Jason.

✧ Minotaur

This was a monster with the head of a bull and the body of a man. King Minos of Crete kept him in an elaborate labyrinth. Each year the king of Athens would send young men and women to Crete to be sacrificed to the monster to ensure peace between their city-states. One year the king's son Theseus volunteered to battle the Minotaur. His victory is a famous Greek legend. Yet, the legend of the Minotaur is based partly in truth. It was discovered that King Minos's palace at Knossos of Crete was filled with many rooms and twisting corridors. Furthermore, a form of entertainment was bull leaping, which consisted of acrobats springing from the beast's back over their horns!

Activities

1. Many more Greek monsters exist in mythology: Cyclops, Chimera, Hydra, Basilisk, Phoenix, etc. (The Basilisk and Phoenix can be found in *Harry Potter and the Chamber of Secrets*.) Choose one Greek monster to research, describe, and draw.

2. Look in the library for books describing these stories of Greek heroes and monsters. Rewrite and illustrate one of these tales.

3. Work with some friends to act out one of the heroic tales involving the Greek monsters. Perform your play for the class.

My Most Memorable Moments

Each Harry Potter book is filled with memorable moments that define his year at Hogwarts. In *Harry Potter and the Sorcerer's Stone*, the Gryffindor House won the house cup and Harry was overjoyed. "It was the best evening of Harry's life, better than winning at Quidditch, or Christmas, or knocking out mountain troll . . . he would never, ever forget tonight." Make a time line of your life based only on those special, memorable events from each year.

Materials

+ A large 12" x 18" (30.4 cm x 45.6 cm) sheet of construction paper
+ tape
+ crayons or markers
+ photographs from home

Directions

1. Cut the sheet of paper in half lengthwise. Tape the two strips together end-to-end.

2. Divide the strip of paper into sections so that you have one section for each year of your life.

3. Label each section with the year and your age.

4. Look through old photo albums and talk to your family about the most memorable events from your life. These could be happenings such as encountering new surroundings, family vacations, and sports events. Include both good and bad memories in your research.

5. Choose one event only from each year to document as the most memorable event for that year. Write about the event on the time line and include a photo if available and appropriate. (Be sure to get permission from your parents before using any photos.)

6. Once finished, decorate the time line.

7. Share your time line with the class and display.

8. Each year, add to your time line to reflect on that year's most memorable event. This is a great family project and a good activity for the changing of the New Year or your birthday.

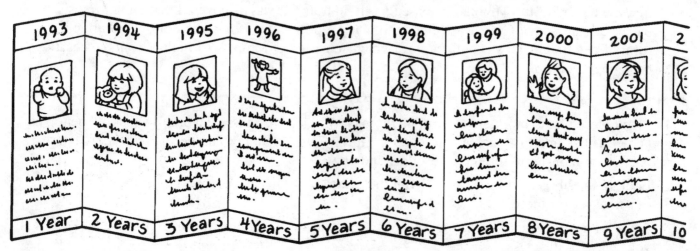

Story Analysis

Answer the questions below after finishing a book to demonstrate your understanding of the story. Use a separate sheet of paper for your responses.

1. Who are the key characters central to the main plot? List each character along with a brief explanation as to why they are important to the plot.

2. When and where is the overall setting for this book?

3. Name at least three specific places/settings that are important to the plot of the story. What major event or revelation happens at each of these places?

4. What is the main conflict that guides the plot and must be resolved by the end of the book?

5. Describe at least three minor conflicts or obstacles that occur during the story that inhibit the characters from solving the main conflict. (These obstacles also help make the story more interesting!)

6. What happens during the climax of the story? Describe the scene in which the characters finally resolve the main conflict.

7. How does the author resolve the story? What happens to the characters in the end?

8. Pretend you are writing a sequel to this book. Based on the end of the story, what do you think will happen to the characters next?

9. Many stories have a theme or message. What do you think the author was trying to convey to you? How does this message apply to your life?

10. Who or what do you find most fascinating in this book? Why?

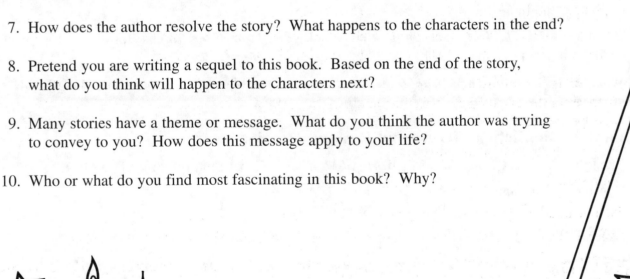

Bibliography of Related Reading

✧ More Books by J.K. Rowling

Harry Potter and the Chamber of Secrets. Scholastic Press, 1999.

Harry Potter and the Prisoner of Azkaban. Scholastic Press, 1999.

✧ Fantasy Fiction—Literature

Baum, Frank L. *The Wizard of Oz.* Ballantine Books, 1986.

Carroll, Lewis. *Alice in Wonderland.* Dover Publications, Incorporated, 1993.

Cooper, Susan. *The Boggart.* Simon & Schuster Children's, 1995.

Dahl, Roald. *Witches.* Farrar, Straus & Giroux, Incorporated, 1983.

Jacques, Brian. *Redwall* (book #1 in Redwall series). Ace Books, 1998.

Lewis, C.S. *The Lion, the Witch, and the Wardrobe* (book #1 in *Chronicles of Narnia* series). HarperCollins Children's Books, 1994.

Osborne, Mary Pope. *Dinosaurs Before Dark* (book #1 in *Magic Tree House* series). Random House, Incorporated, 1992.

Stanton, Mary. *The Road to Balinor* (book #1 in *Unicorns of Balinor* series). Scholastic, Inc., 1999.

Tolkien, J.R.R. *The Fellowship of the Ring* (book #1 in *Lord of the Rings* trilogy). Ballantine Books, Inc., 1981.

Winthrop, Elizabeth. *The Castle in the Attic.* Bantam Doubleday Dell Books for Young Readers, 1986.

✧ Fantasy Nonfiction Picture and Resource Books

Cabat, Erni. *Erni Cabat's Magical World of Monsters.* Cabat Studio Publications, 1992.

D'Aulaire, Ingri and Edgar Parin D'Aulaire. *D'Aulaires' Book of Greek Myths.* Bantam Doubleday Dell Publishing Group, 1980.

Eager, Edward. *Knight's Castle.* Harcourt Brace & Company, 1999.

Evslin, Bernard. *Heroes, Gods, and Monsters of the Greek Myths.* Bantam Books, 1987.

McCaulay, David. *Castle.* Houghton Mifflin, 1983.

Oggins, Robin S. *Castles and Fortresses.* Barnes & Noble Books, 1998.

Osborne, Mary Pope. *Favorite Medieval Tales.* Scholastic, Inc., 1998.

Platt, Richard and Stephen Biesty (Illustrator). *Stephen Biesty's Cross-Sections Castle.* DK Publishing, Incorporated, 1994.

Answer Key

Page 10

Section 1

1. Accept any reasonable answers.
2. Harry's parents were killed and the Dursleys were his only living relatives. Also, Dumbledore didn't want him growing up knowing about his fame until he was old enough to handle it.
3. Harry survived an attack by a powerful dark wizard known as Voldemort. After this attack, Voldemort went away, freeing wizards from his dark spell.
4. Harry has a thin face, knobbly knees, black hair, and bright green eyes. He wears glasses held together by tape and baggy hand-me-down clothes. On his forehead is a thin scar in the shape of a lightening bolt. On the other hand, Dudley has a large pink face, not much neck, small blue eyes, and thick blonde hair.
5. Accept reasonable answers.
6. The letters ask Harry to come to Hogwarts and become a wizard.
7. They go to a little hut on an island in the sea. They don't escape the letters because Hagrid finally delivers the news himself.
8. They are against anything not dull and ordinary. They don't want another wizard in the family.
9. Accept any reasonable answers.
10. Accept any reasonable answers.

Section 2

1. Accept any reasonable answers.
2. They are afraid the Muggles will want to solve all of their problems with magic.
3. Diagon Alley is a shopping area for wizards to get magic supplies. You get there through a pub that only wizards and witches notice on the street. You have to push a special brick on the wall in the alley to make the doorway to the shopping street appear.
4. Accept any reasonable answers.
5. Harry dislikes Draco Malfoy because he is a snob against wizards from poor or Muggle families.
6. Harry's wand contains a feather from the same Phoenix bird as Voldemort's wand.
7. Harry and Ron have had difficult lives and are both unsure about succeeding at Hogwarts.
8. Hufflepuff students are just, loyal, and hard workers. Ravenclaw students are smart, witty, and good at learning. Gryffindor students are brave. Slytherin students are cunning.
9. He knows Voldemort and Draco Malfoy come from Slytherin, as well as all wizards who turned to the dark arts.
10. Harry should beware of Professor Quirrel, Snape, and Draco Malfoy if he is to succeed at Hogwarts.

Section 3

1. Accept any reasonable answers.
2. Accept any reasonable answers.
3. Harry learned that someone was trying to get at whatever Hagrid had taken from the Gringott's vault. He also has the feeling that Hagrid knew why Snape didn't like him, but Hagrid wouldn't tell him.
4. Harry was good at flying on a broom.
5. Quidditch is a wizard sport played with seven players on each team and four balls. The players fly on brooms and try to score points. One ball is used to score points through hoops. Two other balls have a life of their own and they try to knock players off of their brooms. The last ball is very tiny and flies around secretly. Catching this tiny ball ends the game and usually determines the winner.
6. Malfoy baits Harry to get him into trouble. They never actually fought because Harry discovers he is being set up for a trap.
7. Hermione always raises her hand to answer questions, tells everyone how to do spells, criticizes others for not knowing the right answers, and constantly tells others what to do to follow the rules.
8. She becomes a friend by helping Ron and Harry fight off a mountain troll and then lying about it to the teachers.
9. Snape was attacked by the three-headed dog guarding the trap door on the third floor.
10. Someone tried to cast a spell on Harry's broom so that he would fall off during the game.

Section 4

1. Accept any reasonable answers.
2. They are trying to discover the identity of Nicholas Flamel and his connection to the guarded package.
3. Harry got an invisibility cloak. Harry didn't know who sent it, but the note with it said it once belonged to his father.
4. By using the invisibility

Answer Key *(cont.)*

cloak, Harry is able to sneak into the library unseen and discover the Mirror of Erised.

5. The mirror reflected your deepest desires.
6. Nicholas Flamel was Dumbledore's partner and he created the Sorcerer's Stone.
7. It turns any metal to gold and makes the Elixir of Life, a drink that makes you immortal.
8. Accept any reasonable answers.
9. Hagrid is hiding a book about dragons. Dragons could destroy Hagrid and they are illegal. Hogwarts could get into trouble and Hagrid could go to prison.
10. Harry sends an owl to Charlie Weasley in Romania who works with dragons. Charlie's friends come to pick up the dragon. Although the dragon is taken successfully, Harry and Hermione leave the invisibility cloak at the tower and are caught by Filch.

Section 5

1. Accept any reasonable answers.
2. They lost 150 points for their house while trying to get rid of Hagrid's dragon.
3. They have to go into the forbidden forest with Hagrid to find out what has been killing the unicorns.
4. They see a cloaked figure drinking the blood of a dead unicorn. They know Voldemort was there trying to get the stone and kill Harry.
5. They play a tune on the flute to put the dog to sleep.
6. They have to untangle some Devil's Snare from around their bodies, capture a flying key to open a door, play a live game of chess, step over

a troll, and logically determine the right potion to drink to get through the black flames and on to the Mirror of Erised.

7. Professor Quirrel is working with Voldemort.
8. Harry gets the stone by looking into the Mirror of Erised. His greatest desire at that moment was just to find the stone, not use it, and Dumbledore had cast a spell to that effect. Quirrel is unable to attack Harry for the stone because Harry was protected by his mother's love. So, although Quirrel tried to kill Harry, Dumbledore arrives in time to save him from harm.
9. Accept any reasonable answers.
10. Accept any reasonable answers.

Page 31

1. Dudley
2. dragon
3. forbidden forest
4. Albus Dumbledore
5. Vernon Dursley
6. Ron Weasley
7. Sir Nicholas de Mimsy
8. Diagon Alley
9. Professor McGonagall
10. Voldemort
11. Fluffy
12. Bloody Baron
13. Harry Potter
14. Severus Snape
15. Draco Malfoy
16. Professor Quirrel
17. Petunia Dursley
18. centaur
19. Hermione Granger
20. Hogwarts
21. unicorn
22. Gringotts
23. Neville Longbottom
24. Peeves

Witches and Wizards—Albus Dumbledore, Professor McGonagall, Voldemort, Professor Quirrel, Severus Snape

Students—Harry Potter, Ron Weasley, Hermione Granger, Neville Longbottom, Draco Malfoy

Muggles—Dudley Dursley, Vernon Dursley, Petunia Dursley

Creatures—dragon, centaur, unicorn, Fluffy

Ghosts—Peeves, Sir Nicholas de Mimsy, Bloody Baron

Places—Diagon Alley, forbidden forest, Hogwarts, Gringotts

Page 32

Matching

1. h	6. g
2. f	7. a
3. b	8. c
4. i	9. d
5. e	10. j

True/False	Sequence
1. true	a. 4
2. false	b. 1
3. false	c. 5
4. true	d. 2
5. false	e. 3

Page 36

Gryffindor: red and gold—lion—brave—Harry Potter, the Weasleys, Hermione Granger, Neville Longbottom, Professor McGonagall, Nearly Headless Nick (Sir Nicholas de Mimsy) the ghost

Hufflepuff: black and yellow—badger—just, loyal, hard workers—Fat Friar ghost

Ravenclaw: blue and yellow—eagle—smart, witty, able to learn

Slytherin: green and silver—serpent/snake—cunning—Draco Malfoy, Crabbe, Goyle, Professor Snape, Voldemort, the Bloody Baron ghost.